We're the Same

Visit us on the Web!
randomhousekids.com
SesameStreetBooks.com
www.sesamestreet.org

Educators and librarians, for a variety of teaching tools, visit us at RHTeachersLibrarians.com

ISBN 978-1-5247-7056-3 (trade) — ISBN 978-1-5247-7057-0 (ebook)

MANUFACTURED IN CHINA
10 9

WE'RE DIFFERENT,
WE'RE THE SAME

By Bobbi Jane Kates

Illustrated by Joe Mathieu

Random House 🏠 New York

We're different.

Our noses are different.

We're the same.

Our noses are the same.

They breathe and sniff
and sneeze and whiff.

FLOWERS
FOR SALE

Our hair is different.

Our hair is the same.

It grows on us in several places.
It warms our heads and frames our faces.

Our mouths are different.

Our mouths are the same.

Their lips form the words we say
and smile when it's a happy day.

Our skin is different.

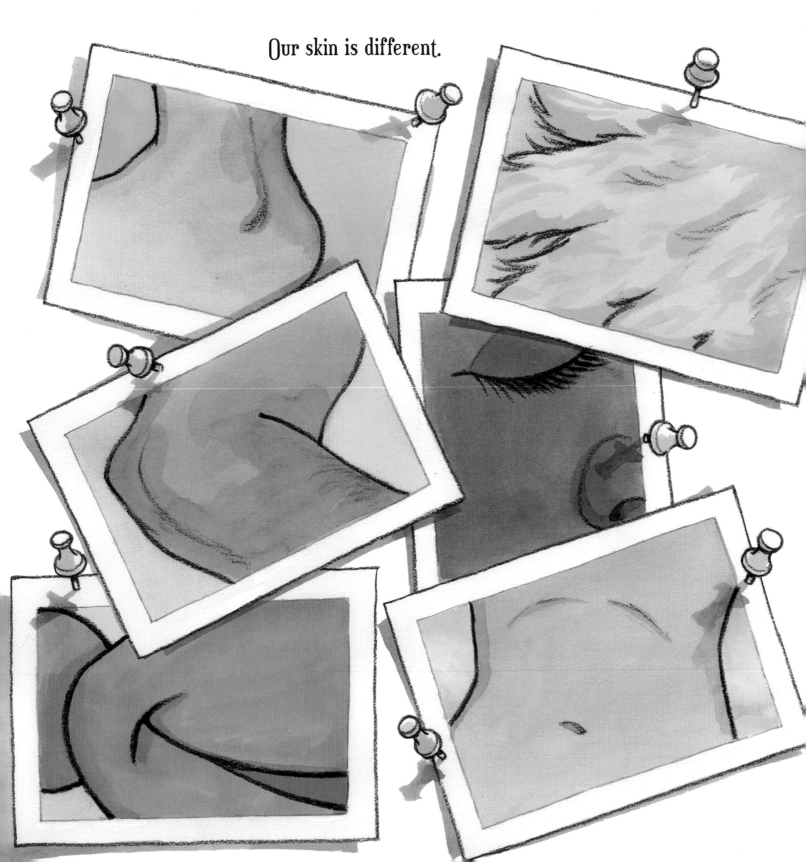

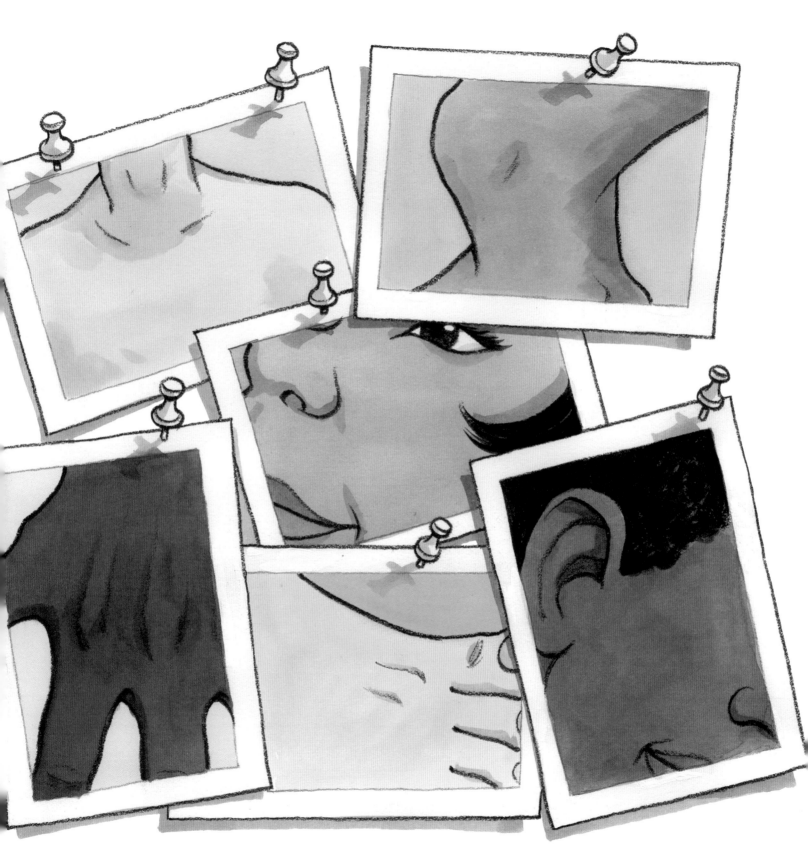

Our skin is the same.

It tells us something's cold or hot,
or wet or dry. It knows a lot.

Muscles and bones are wrapped inside it. We
all have blood and skin to hide it!
It keeps in warmth. It keeps out dirt.
It warns us so we don't get hurt.

Our eyes are different.

Our eyes are the same.

They see, they blink,
they weep, they wink.

Our bodies are different.

Our bodies are the same.

They stretch and bend and work and play.
They all need food and rest each day.
They dance and wriggle and ride a bike.
They might look different, but they're alike!

Our feelings are different.

Our feelings are the same.

Lonely, worried, scared, excited—
happy, loving, glad, delighted.

We're the same.
We're different.

That's what makes the world such fun. Many
kinds of people, not just one!
A rainbow would be boring
if it were only green or blue.
What makes a rainbow beautiful
is that it has every hue.
So aren't you glad you look like *you*?

We're different.
We're the same.

We're wonderful!